The Lost Sea

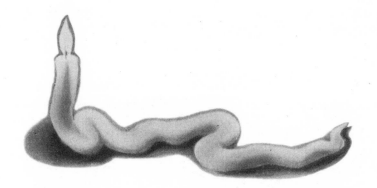

The Lost Sea

For Bill,

Keith Flynn

thanks for listening to my ragged blues

Keith Flynn

Iris Press
Oak Ridge, TN
www.irisbooks.com

The author wishes to thank Fred Chappell, Thomas Rain Crowe, and Robert West for their helpful suggestions in the final editing process of this collection. Special thanks to Rob Amberg for the inspiration of his work and his abiding friendship.

COVER ARTIST:
René Magritte: *Meditation* (1937)
Oil on Canvas (34 x 39 cm)
Courtesy of the Edward James Foundation,
Chichester, Sussex, UK

BOOK DESIGNER:
Robert B. Cumming, Jr.

~

Library of Congress Cataloging-in-Publication Data

Flynn, Keith.
  The lost sea / Keith Flynn.
      p. cm.
  ISBN 0-916078-51-5 (alk. paper)
  1. Title.
  PS3556.L875 L67 2000
  811'.6—dc21
                                    00-010345

ACKNOWLEDGMENTS

The author wishes to thank the following editors and journals
where these poems first appeared:

Asheville Poetry Review: "Lines Composed Upon The Isle of Palms,"
    "The Acquired Inability to Escape, Inverted"
Bombay Gin: "The Manneporte," "Brace's Rock"
Bone and Flesh: "The Pink River Dolphins of Peru"
The Cafe Review: "Narcissisyphus"
The Carolina Quarterly: "Rasputin at the Rapture"
The Colorado Review: "The Paper-Maker's Wave"
The Cuirt Journal (Ireland): "Drought Horse," "Principia"
Earth and Soul: The Kostroma Anthology (Russia): "A Psalm for
    Camille"
Defined Providence: "The Bat"
Independence Boulevard: "Conspiracy Theory," "Exit the Ballets
    Russes"
Lonzie's Fried Chicken: "Dreaming of Segovia"
Lurch Magazine: "The Borderland," "Two Generations of Snow"
Main Street Rag: "Agama," "The Last Barrier of Sex"
New Millennium Writing: "Rudy," "The Whale in Winter"
New York Waste: "The Voluptuous Horror of Karen Black"
Nexus: "Critical Mass"
The Nomad: "The Mayor of Antarctica"
Now and Then: "Lessons In Hunger"
Oyster Boy Review: "The Power of Movement In Plants,"
    "Undertow"
Pine Mountain Sand & Gravel: "Sunny Limbo"
Poems and Plays: "The Death of the Poet"
Poetry Wales: "Thirty Years After My Lai"
Rattle: "The Diaspora of Steven Manners"
The Southern Poetry Review: "A Call to Remember"
Third Lung Review: "Exegesis"
Wild Mountain Times: "Granny Grunt," "The Tree of Life"
W.P. Journal (Ireland): "Death Is A Fiction of Stone"

For Aimee

Who knows

A Deep Intelligence of Peace
An introduction by Donald Revell

Sound transposes distance to the near. Thus music, the most radically local of the arts, is always and instantly universal. I imagine that is why Henry Thoreau, America's neighborhood cosmologist, followed, in *Walden*, a brief chapter on "Reading" with a much longer consideration of "Sounds." The bells of Concord, transmuted by the trees of Walden's woods, were nearer and more godly to Henry than to most folks in the town. The difference? The townsman heard bells. Henry heard worlds.

Keith Flynn is a musician by profession: a substantial performing and recording artist. In his *poetry*, his music does not merely contribute; it continues. Flynn's poetic vision *is* a music, immediate, large, and cosmologically local, wherever it happens and however it happens to transpire. In *The Lost Sea*, language is cleansed of second-hand representations and once again acquires, like the Concord bells, sacred presence to one and to any *one* inclined by soul, like Henry Thoreau, like Keith Flynn, to hear.

True music is never solitary, is always accompanied by the world. Flynn welcomes such blessed company in the kinetic simultaneities of his craft. A poem such as "The Paper-Maker's Wave" is thus able to enact an Augustinian universal in stanzas whose centers are everywhere, whose circumferences are nowhere.

> In the region of mysterious mosses
> and wild genista, among the almond trees,
> you are a velvet fish flying.
> Your silent impenetrable dignity

is impossible to ridicule,
as invisible as pollen.
Wide eyes in a sudden August rain,
the width of a veil from oblivion.

The stars are swimming in this wind,
an incandescent trellis of flowers
in the quiet avalanche of time.
Like the paper-maker's wave crested
between his hands, the wind flips the sky
and welcomes the lake's serene surface,
unmoved by swallow or salmon strike,
a vast shimmering carpet of silver flies.

The effect of such transformations is, as in Walden woods, not chaos, but serenity. The world is a dissonance at peace with itself. This is the dear purpose of much of *The Lost Sea*: peace. An aching need for peace—between lovers, between parents and children, between life and death—lifts these poems to their highest registers, and there peace plays.

Yet I do not mean to suggest that Flynn is in some kind of flight from the violence of the real. Just as all music is first percussive and a clamor, so are his ideals of peace rooted in a deep understanding of conflict. In "The Diaspora of Steven Manners," this understanding itself becomes visionary.

There will come an evening, I am certain,
while the herds of turtles
row towards their death
with muffled oars, when the last convertible
cruises the beach stuffed with bikinis,

and the last sister is held defenseless
by her wrists on the wrinkled shore.

A fog of men, torn on the strings
of their own instrument,
will make a perfect scream of forgetting,

their progeny glued like smug honey
to the rocks, in the twilight
of dungeons, passing through the slalom
of their automatic doom
on skis of meat.

Emerald sea-flowers will emerge,
their heads ablaze in human forms
and trying to speak.
But then their tortured eyes will meet,
cloaked in feathery remembrance,
of lovers thrown from towers,

of loneliness deep as a needle
in the scattered engines of sleep.
And they will walk slowly together
from the Celtic maze upon a crippled street,
its pathway littered with marble Apollos,
overgrown by the gallows of the beginning.

Flynn's dazzling simultaneities and candor are much more than
praiseworthy. They are, if our poetry is not to disappear into an
academic echo of itself, crucial. Flynn everywhere avers that
everything, which is nothing less than History, entirely
demands both our presence and our present attention. This is
the moral law of music: to be heard, it must be listened to, not
upon clever reflection, but NOW. Flynn has no time or truck
with irony, and for this I honor him. Our age is deformed and
disabled by its bad equation of intelligence with irony. In a
masterpiece, "The Fatigue of Post-Modern Irony," Flynn
rejects the bad equation and breathes a pure clear music into
words.

If I
could
speak
to you
as clearly
dear reader
as the
moon speaks
to the hill
I would
lay my
cheek
against
your cheek
and say
this is all
we are
every
blue breath
viewed
from afar
takes
something
from
this
world.

This is endlessly intelligent and wholly embodied. This is no trick. These are words on the line. These are Flynn's words on the line and indistinguishable from body. The current of *The Lost Sea* is a "blue breath," human and unlimited. As Keith Flynn has done and is doing still, we may trust ourselves to it, body and soul.

CONTENTS

THE FATIGUE OF POST-MODERN IRONY

STILL LIFE WITH DELIRIUM

The Great Spring of the West

"...the time must come when the powerfully elastic spring of our rapidly increasing numbers shall fill up our wide spread territory with a dense population...the great safety valve of the west will be closed against us..."

—Thomas Dew, 1836

GRANNY GRUNT

The river makes its own decisions,
independent of gravel or gravity
or Granny Grunt's sweet coaxing
with her two feet stuck in the middle
of her new swimming hole.

Her long gray braid dips into the water
as she crouches to cup a drink
with both hands and whisper,
slow down, rest with me a moment
behind the dam, roll me around.

But water seeks, undivided, headlong
without caution, cannot be filled
or foraged and sleeps with its own kind.
The dam will leak, shudder and fall away;
serene will be the remnants here.

But tomorrow on the shore, after the squall
and ripped release, Granny will hold
two rocks in her hands and begin,
from one side and then the other,
the reconstruction of her dam.

The Whale in Winter

Socked in by the fog,
the rain's spidery remnants
chase themselves across the windows.
The red maple flames in the wind.
All the Halloween leaves answer
in their angry skins, shuddering
down as if from a quiver of arrows.
An eagle's single purpose dips
him in pockets of moldy air,
swimming through spores and parachutes,
his Picasso eye bent to the ground.
Thunder sleeps and drifts,
bulges in the vapor, but does not bark.

Back against the wall, a magazine
is thumbed open with a ship
in glorious relief chasing whales
through the gravy-gray sea.
On the upper deck, the unruly
virtually cyber rusting wives
are guiding their men
with Prozac wafers and crooked fingers
dabbed in clam sauce.
The portholes scream instructions
and everybody stands.
An exotic Alaskan dinner is prepared,
codfish cakes deep-fried in antelope fat.
The toilets start laughing, gurgling
like secret agents and the wild wives
simplify, tin-tough and creaking
through the plaster statues of horses
straining to listen. The fizz of champagne

foaming in their cheeks, the women,
beneath chandeliers of wisteria,
steam the deck with frosty glances.

Two Olympic walkers scissor their hips
down Chapel Ave. on the holiday deck
through the boggy red power ties.
1600 women die each day
from pregnancy or childbirth,
one says to the other.
A new cold war is coming.
The sun plays peek-a-boo
between smokestacks as the pendulums
twist back together,
bleeding on their cornucopia.
My wisdom teeth are killing me.
My son's fiancée is a cunt.
Jonathan thinks I am so stupid.
In a world of sharp corners,
the past keeps running back to meet us
or as Faulkner said,
it's not even past,
it's the other things, the odd shapes
of intentions, it's how we mock God.

We all want to join our lover's play
in the first act, not the third,
to overflow in the wake of a whisper
entirely different, open all night
like a burning map's still life
of lesions and passageways.
The ship tilts north
between herds of singing humpbacks.
Only the males sing, their slick trunks
hard and thick as redwoods,

rising skyward from a funnel of sea,
flippers out-stretched like the arms of Christ.
They moan and cry, improvising notes
as the currents whip against the haunted tribes.
Mammals that never sleep and cannot rest,
fighting eternally to the surface for breath.

Imagine the body without repressions,
the jazz and sizzle, the waves breaking
around the hole of our open song
and all the world steady
and the blast of broad shadows sprayed.
But the black holes in our bodies
open resplendent aerobic bruises
and our blood ticks down.
First the bed is stale and then poisonous,
the steps strung out; the parlor
upholstery ambers and one chair
becomes as convenient as the other,
a deplorable lacuna of velour.
The whale only sings in winter
and then no song at all;
it's the strange topography
that shame sets up, in the darkness,
beneath the luxurious ice,
a porch light and a bubble of air
that fits your head exactly.

THE BORDERLAND

The chimney for the nuclear
reactor in Odessa, Delaware
spews empty steam into the air.

Pretty Ruth Tingle is clerk
of the peace, wanders the historic
district with her Shar Pei on a leash,

lost in that yawn of space
where the eyes of our animals
stare blankly back at us.

On a quiet Monday, she is
watching the wolfish river
claw past the town's moody bridge.

Ms. Tingle says men are machines
made of numbers and teams,
just bales and bales of sand.

The voters agree, their inertia
decreed by the government's
blood on their hands.

The river's stem is sturdy
but slim, where it divides
the borderland.

THE BAT

Amber twilight, a juvenile bat
is chasing mosquitoes in a clear
patch of sky, like a broken kite
being churned by savage currents,
its jerks and titters leave
a manic imprint, changing, as the light
itself changes and flutters invisibly away.

The centuries tirelessly swim, friends fade,
lovers betray the gentle swoop of their bodies
and the air blows up, leaving a trail
of new beginnings, like ice found
by satellites on the surface of Mars.
The death masks among the craters
form blind eyes like machine gun fire staring
back down the barrels of our telescopes.

A comet lends its water
to the lake of history,
behind two ghost moths mating
fluorescently in the moonlit heights,
drooping like wintergreen feathers,
elegant and milky-white,
searching like anxious parachutes
for anonymous disturbances in the field.

The planets rest their elbows on the trolley
stars, watching our boats that bulge
and heave in the wake of steel.
Burdened with footprints, I hear
the broken sounds jutting into the dark.
My head steers, like a wheel
on a rail, swallowing sparks.

The Tree of Life

This morning, after much nausea and many sordid dreams,
a tree sprouted from my navel and pushed me down,
its roots spreading in every direction,
like a giant snake that had escaped
from my spleen and shot into the sky.
A grove of sycamores shivered in the early light,
the tentacles of the sun probing their muscled shoulders,
scarlet tumbleweeds shining like blood on the silos.
I watched their jewelled souls take flight,
struggling toward noon through vines of clouds,
and held the shaft of the spear
that had shattered my body with both hands,
until the invisible flow that is a man
passed like a river from my eyes.

Full to brimming with lichens and poetry,
the dream of my death was a circle
sucked and sharpened by herds of deer
and every illusion that I inhaled
became the incense of the forest,
a residue of feathers and skeletons
gathered in a mortal coil around my heart.
The scream that I suppressed was proof
of my deliverance and my denial as well,
making sacred the burden of thunder,
dissolving the smoky undeciphered delirium of my life.

Stunned but fully conscious, I watched as a hawk
passed over me and dropped its prey,
a field mouse with its head missing.
My tongue was an alien, sticking out like a tombstone,
and with it I licked all the fingers of my free hand

like a cat one by one and opened my mind slowly
as if drugged beneath a surgeon's knife
to see what I had become.
A hairy mound of earth I was,
feeling the pinprick of diamonds all along my spine,
my belly ruling a vast reserve of petroleum,
my shoulders transmogrified, shielding
an indifferent cavern of translucent bones.

Locked in a labyrinth of duty, my legs drained
into the river, holding my feet firm
in the rising catacombs of salmon-colored mud,
the domain of the snapper and his brood,
the old chipped father with his beard of hooks.
Powerless to rise, the rituals of breath were all I owned
as the mountains wrinkled and pressed down
and the buried lives beneath me made their repeated vows
to the sun, their voices in my hips, their birds bursting
out of my chest as I listened to the engines on patrol
push through the valley, leathery cats loitering in the shadows,
all of us, waiting for the loggers to come.

Lines Composed Upon the Isle of Palms

Across the boardwalk
the skates rattle and click
like sewing machines.
The sun is breaking,
a curve of silence
dipping its blade into the horizon.
Coolly gliding past on the great divide,
its trembling hieroglyphic eyes
rise like roses from the harbor,
forming a hive of sherbet light.
Like hurricanes tied silently
at the tail, quarried in a bowl
of shadows, the crazed currents
suckle at the cratered inlet,
whirlpools spinning round the spiny legs
of crabs, their silt hair melted golden,
frenzied in the explosion of morning.

What is a moral animal?
Which doors are locked
in the body's mansion,
in the talisman of rooms
tied like the bridges
stringing these islands one by one
out along the wrists of the sea,
travelling the same destination
from vessel to vessel
in a hundred different ways?

The universe is elastic, expanding,
not breathing, mind you,
but the shape of time and space

are always changing.
The great policeman of the past,
the speed of light
blows its billion heartbeats
across the billboards of the sky.
Time counts and keeps on counting,
slower as it goes, its Big Bang
falling to pieces, ticking on frog legs
in a vast bathtub of Death,
stony invisible like the dome
of the synagogue grown bald in the sun.

Like the green iris
of a giant eye,
the circle of trees flex
against the hard city limits,
ignoring the neon trickle
where the gas pumps stand
side by side,
making their proper salute.
Between the suburban outcrops
where the trucks are dumping their fill,
there is a line you must not cross,
where the barbaric water is turned away,
where the waving leaves,
the to and fro of lithe schooners,
the facets of the bee's wing
roll and unroll
by any means necessary.
The sea washes. The pine trees swish.

What sprawl is hidden
behind the tall hedges?
The ceremonious trains whine past
the loose fences, vacant lots,

yards sagging under the bare backs
of iron pipes where Joseph and Mary,
soberly dressed for their Nativity scene,
are leading the Christ child
on his black donkey.
One elephant, whose ears have eroded,
lags behind, raising his hopeful
trunk toward heaven.

Vast rooftops revolve in the distance
like pinwheels, stirring a whiff of violets.
What was once the field is now the desert.
What was once the desert is now the sea.
On the edge of collapse,
as silence surprises the waterfall,
the exclamation mark of the lighthouse
shudders in its first decay,
its shuttered windows unable to bear
the traffic of seclusion or the ache
of the pornographic beach,
littered with happy inevitable violence.
Below the antique light,
the winding staircase gathers its dust
and feels the music of chance
riding up and down its stem
of darkening melodies.
Among the wreckage, eels stuffed
with electrons pounce on insects
the size of stars.
What we are, I know, is water.
What we choose to make is love.

THE PINK RIVER DOLPHINS OF PERU

(for Octavio Paz)

The pink river dolphins of Peru
are more myth now than reality,
but some still exist,
radishes of petrified laughter,
ashes in the river roots
shocked into music.
Whatever is not stone is light,
like the pythia said, preaching
in the troubled body's lost horizon.
Music is a blouse on the moon,
unzipping her shadow
and stepping out into blossom.

Once the pink river dolphins of Peru
were revered emperors from another world,
entering the village on human legs
with strange smiles and stories
from the Amazonian depths.
300 pounds and nine feet high,
they stepped out barefoot
on the edge of a knife.
Their sparkling teeth made
from the stones of the deep,
their heads spun round 360 degrees.

When history awakens, the water is dead,
they said, clicking and hissing, but we tore
the night apart dreaming of music,
crashing through towers of birds.

Rooms of ghosts watched us from the other shore,
unloading their taxis behind trees of time
where the sky made from tears walks the land,
footsteps of stones in the invisible afternoon.
Music is a moral law whose great heart springs
open like a net unrolling from its loom.

Between silence and music
are the pink river dolphins of Peru,
broken by men into factories of air,
architectural equations staggering in the sun.
Drunk on the tawny meridians,
the planets ride like fire
across the scorpion-dazzled field.
In the river of hands, one pink snout
is lifting and one child disbelieving, kneels.
With the mud for a mother the beast is gone.
Only the mist we drink is real.

The Power of Movement in Plants

Something went wrong on the operating table
                    as the scientists
                                        struggled to design
            a more contemporary daisy
and the people outside were peeking in the window
                                on the prowl for celebrities
            and three Haitians
                        with hands like feathers
            were playing hide the pea
stringing pearls together by their hope of paradise
            and everyone leaned rhyming forward
            ready to audition the daisy
                    and one scientist filled with savage thoughts
of apostasy kept screaming *Garbo Zombies Mambo*
            like some kind of weird mantra
                        and a picket line of erotic children
            danced in a circle
saying everything unfinished is a kindred spirit
                        and snapdragons groaned
            in the brawl of a dry thicket
            and critics with honeymoon elbow
cruised the corridors in complete confusion
                            saying ten days before Christmas
                            Hollywood needs the daisy
                            and the tension was unbearable
as scientists built on the will of the people
                        presiding over the death of history
                        saints of reason lusting in earnest
            whispered centuries of rebellion
            agnostics in their blind alleys trembled
                and from its deep murky well
the great daisy like a ghost woman whose face was the sun

issued forth
                              its enormous petals unfolding
                 and crickets like dark angels
leaped singing from the buildings in ruin
and the kingdom of flowers hardened against the shadows
                 and the roar
                              of the daisy
                 was louder than a thousand dawns
           and the sound of its voice was a scar.

LANDSCAPE WITH TRAIN AFTER MERTON

"Out of the towers of water
Four or five mountains come walking
To see the little monks' graves."

In the Sun and the Rain

Sound brings us to our senses
says Thoreau and so does shame,
walking on little claw feet
with its ears wide open,
learning to fall faster
through the forsythia-whips
and the vast carelessness
of the underbrush.

The firmament is moving
beyond the power grid
and the radar screen.
Rhythm, with its romantic readiness,
affirms the supernal oleander
and chiming hibiscus.

When the sun sings
its morning aubade
like a comet shaking loose
its long hair in the inky dark
and giggles across the frosted stream,
the orchids come crying,
holding their white bells
overhead to be kissed.

When that same sun
plunges its lance
into the eyes of a lone German shepherd
sitting like a senator
on the promontory by the gate,
the canticles of the crow
take greater precedence.
All the hollow wind shrieks
through the golden leaves.
The cane fields lift
their reeds and play.

I've stood on a mountainside
in the late afternoon,
winded and worn and heard,
roaming on the green air
that filled my lungs,
a train whistle and the low
rolling rumble of iron wheels,
slow at first, the bass notes
sharpened on the brittle
autumn leaves and then the air
shaking loose its cymbals.

From ten miles away
the airborne music,
the voice that pierced
the wilderness, running faster
than water inexorably west.
Goldfinches the color of honey
blow through the dandelion globes,
out of the gap-toothed grin
of the bearded corn,
wheeling wildly as heaven
and earth collide, bickering

with the mockingbirds
and the bees' steady drizzle,
no louder than a shower of pins,
settling in the muzzy bouquets,
startled now and then
by a woodpecker's antiphons,
hammering and resting
in a glen of oaks.

The greasy clouds slide across
the slippery harbor, gathering
the day in sheaves of fire.
Blazing hay disappears
with the sound of the train
that scatters on the barn roof
like sparks rattling through
the rigging of a ship.

The deep cedars bend
as the squirrels trapeze and dip.
The silver poplars sigh.
Behind the empty rails
still humming, mourning
like oyster shells
against the brass traffic
of the train,
the mountains come walking.

In the growing dark
I scream and sing and cheer,
knowing that the brain
like a star peering from its hole,
dragging its echo behind,
does not naturally hear.

Learning to listen may
take a thousand years.

The black notes bog the reliquaries
like coal dust on a lens.
The mountains come walking,
looming over the factory's
thrumming dynamos, the jig and clatter
like spoons rolling under the focused
agony of the train, ecclesiastical mosaics
gather like a locust swirl and scatter
the commerce of the windows.
The lamps have darkened.
Mechanized machetes rise and fall.
The mountains come walking.

THE ENCHANTED LOOM

"History that should be a left hand to us, as of a violinist, we bind up with prejudice, warping it to suit our fears as Chinese women do their feet."

—William Carlos Williams

I

The Loom Transfigured

Brace's Rock

(for Fitz Hugh Lane)

At high tide I tumble
out into the sun, watch the cars
put an end to tourist season,
speeding inland toward the mountains
where the hawks circle leisurely,
not like here in the tricky heat
where the gulls are crying and diving
and pluck fish like eyebrows
from the cloudy face of the sea.

Blown by a gentle wind,
the ocean performs its grand jetés,
here in Gloucester
where the crippled Lane
painted his last abandoned boat.
Poisoned by an apple of Peru,
he drew pictures better
than he made shoes,
storms and sunsets dressed in red,
with the determination to detail
each separate wave
and to give that wave a life.
Lane's last ship had no sail
and rested gasping on its side.
The rocks from the shore
gathered in a solemn prayer
and the horizon was one color,
a final glorious flowering of light.

From that fixed point
where the harbor is torn
in the expected manner,
where the cannibal bands of gulls
perform their charming tournaments
and death intersects with the dance.
They laugh and fall silent as they dive
and are washed toward the farthest shore,
gripped in the soft slow erosion of courage.
Their random cries leading
the ghosts from the wreckage,
like sentries drifting above
the incomparable geometry of the deep.

THE MANNEPORTE

(for Claude Monet)

When Michelangelo struck the knee
of Moses and bade the stone to speak,
he knew that nothing in Nature can endure.
Who was he to question the love of ruin
or the relentless efficiency, so amazed
at the courage of color that he would
never attempt to paint it, only duplicate
its forms, the throbbing knots and gristle
of anatomy books, the tempest poured from
the distances of mirrors or the sea
sighing back again its muscular nocturnal.

What lethargic winding coil raises its veil
when the remains of April lurch in the wild lotion
of geese streaming home, the heart suddenly stopped
and listening to itself? Abruptly lifted up,
what underground shadow spreads its water blossoms
of blue lilies further down than a stream
may penetrate, forgetting the miles it must go?
Gorged and unassailable, fastened beneath
our hump of security, all the world exists
on the tops of our boots, trudging ambitiously above
the business occurring in the veins of the earth.

Beneath the fox-scented moss and silent toss
of creatures, the husks and salt and withered sea roots,
the cosmology is submerged inside a towering cathedral
where the sculptor swims and wrestles
the marble God struggling anxiously to surface.
Descartes dreamed a clock and Newton

cooked it into motion. Dali painted it
dripping upon a rock which did not move.
Monet stripped and placed his ear against the sheer
rock face of Giverny, knowing that the nature
of light exists in a vast region of empty space
and that the nucleus is invisible.

We have no tendencies really, just as the wind
cannot be measured with any great probability;
yet the planet of Saturn still slowly disappears
inside its rings and the cliff, reaching
for the fish uprooted in a storm, calls out
to its counterparts and rots away.
Like God's cornea frozen before Monet
in the hole of Manneporte, an outline
of the wind's transparent history perfectly
whispered its tiny hiccup into him,
spraying his gaze into the soft deep belly
of the heavens, clinging to the fibers of comets,
nourished like a divine spider on the infectious
barnacles and ancient morsels that the sun sucks up,
mildew and minerals, acids, gasses, alkalines,
all the aphrodisiacs of space.

The face of his beloved Camille,
feathery and motionless, sweetly
beckoned him to the edges.
But a huge wave swept he and his canvas
into the Black Sea's static crease.
He took in his hands the downpour,
gray and violet, and ground it
into the shaking white canvas.
The cliffs swelled against
the boiling tide, blue and pink sun
flung its arms into the fray.

The tiny fishing boats disappeared
into the nets of that unfriendly foam.
A fugitive flood of yellow tones
came frothing from his children,
standing bewildered on the shore,
buttressed with webs of writhing flowers,
the verve of light in all things
and always green with violent delirium,
and drowned in animal praise.
The painter was ripped free of earth
and floated, twisting against the leaden sky.
Blown through the howling cauldron,
he swam in the needle's eye.

Rasputin at the Rapture

As God collapses,
I fill the hole
with poetry.
Out of the forest,
out of the mud-splattered peasantry,
I am on all fours
in a golden kitchen
speaking in tongues.

It is the fate
of my imagination
to be implicated
in this dirty business,
graves clogged
with diamonds
and treachery.
The poorest children
have no fear of failure.
We are surrounded by it
and readily dream
of driving the black
carriage of time
straight into the heavens.

The wheels already seem
to be set upon their path
and greased
with remarkable honesty.
I collect their women.
I tick in their ears
like a horrible clock,
a gnat's breath

upon the neck
of the country.

The Russian soul is built
with nervous splendor,
blind allegiance
and cruelty, like ore
rotting unretrieved
in the veins of the mine.
Its dust boils
in our beards and our eyes,
guarded by a magic camera.

We hammer in that frame,
despite the digging
and the slogans.
The enemy is everywhere
like a web
and just as silent.
To be a worker
when one is a peasant,
to be at one
with the Tsar even better,
floating on a bed

of ostrich feathers,
rolling in a well-lit room
and smearing the breasts
of the body politic
with perfumed jellies.
My words are pearls
and gather skin.
The sky opens.
I walk backward
against the river.

The Voluptuous Horror of Karen Black

She is a technicolor trout, red and swollen,
sweeping through the nets of stained glass windows.
Surrounded by conspiracies, they gather
in the churches to touch her,
mastered by her nonchalance,
the seductive art of pushing away.
Karen Black inhabits a hole in the air,
where flesh instructs and echoes guide
the mirrors of her mind underground,
where the living is done, with microphones
and a soul train, because in the white prisons
of the sun, there are walls and wires
between us, wars and remnants of war.

Jesse Helms is afraid of Karen Black
because she can save us.

In the undulating orb of her body,
her tangled black mane drenched with sap,
all the acrobats of time are sheltered,
slithering cool as jelly
beneath the lampposts of her arms.
The earth rotates on its wobbly axis,
filled with gutters of limbs and embryos,
Himalayas of ennui and disgust.
Just when it seems that we have seen too much,
tonight, deep in the heart of Manhattan,
Karen Black is dancing us free,
prancing like a pony,
up to her neck in blood.

Rudy

The dancer, a swan among men,
sullen, forbidding and tender,
bowed eighty-nine times in Vienna
like a butterfly with his wings afire,
caught in the rigging of a fateful leap.
There is no end to the sudden fury
of sterile perfection or the monuments
of mirrors or the sea perfectly
lending its agony to the shore.

Fifty years may be lost in the maze
of a moment, when the final *pas de deux*
sparkles perfectly in the dancer's aging legs
and his eyes fix the audience
in that instant with a superior
triumphant gaze, asking;
How could you think my time has come?
How would you push me off the stage?

The howl of the sea and the howl of a man
are different voices often heard together.
The dancer knew he was dying.
For ten years he had known
that one day he would no longer
astonish himself, that the water
of voices stirring the sea to leap
would become still and the perpetual
I am, despite the fireworks,
would be usurped by the virus
ticking like a bomb in his blood.

We belong to the earth,
but our bodies are wild.
Mortified by the double ensemble,
the dancer rushed to shorten his sails,
sneaking into Central Park *en pointe*,
under the cover of twilight,
thirsty to glimpse the adoring haunted
creatures thrown from the volcano,
desperate for the surge
of inevitable dynamite that might
split apart this gruesome crucible.

Others might die at his hands,
this he knew, but to swing
on the wings of the kingfisher,
would that not be something,
an enchantment intensified
by mutually assured destruction?
The dancer knew he was dying,
but being a god, he abjured.

SUNNY LIMBO

Smoking hash and drinking Frangelico
in Birmingham, Alabama
with David Allan Coe.
If Porter Wagoner and Hulk Hogan
had a baby and sent it to prison,
this would be it.
David talks the talk
and knows the eternity
born of continual contemplation.
All jails are the same, he says,
be it Jersey, Miami or New Mexico.
It's no coincidence that poor people
line the halls of Death Row.
Money has a sixth sense.
It stands you at attention
and turns you around.
It measures your waistline
with a mocking glance.

The TV like a picture frame,
sways in the background,
an Elvis impersonator in Vegas
doing a Hair Club For Men
commercial with a red jumpsuit
and the perfectly proportioned
paunch of the late period.
I changed the face
of country music twice, David says,
and now my enemies grow fat
on what I've left behind.
He turns around and looks me
in the eye. *Sit down boy,*

you're making me nervous.
Most businessmen, he continues,
are uneasy in the presence of magic.

But David has a real magic show,
a dummy named Sonny
sits on his lap
and his lips move when he talks.
It ain't a circus without the tents,
David says to no one in particular.
And the kids keep coming
to hear the perfect country song,
to watch the rhinestones
disappear one by one
until his Cheshire smile,
twisted by weather and bourbon,
is all that remains,
floating behind the microphone
without possibility of parole,
his sovereign rebel baritone
judging the wicked & afflicted alike.

NARCISSISYPHUS

Rolling a blue mirrored ball
    up a mountain of smoke,

every Charlie Parker solo was a struggle,
each note rescued and released,

    like strangled fish
    bursting into air.

Weighted as he was by the black backdrop
of history or the tumble of a clumsy snare,

    his great gnarled hands
caressing the buttons on her silver neck,

    to reveal the wind's worth,
    the nothing that was there.

The Painter as Mantis Sings the Blues

I came stillborn into this world.
Don Salvador blew cigar smoke
into my little pinched nostrils.
Terrified angels flushed out of my eyes
like Apaches charging on white mustangs,
screaming *Wake up, niño, wake up.*
My father took me in his cape and wrapped me
in its folds. I was always hungry.
I learned to walk by pushing a tin
of biscuits. I learned to paint
by watching my father sketch

dining room pictures, partridges and rabbits,
pigeons and lilies. By the age of thirteen,
my birds and bulls came alive.
Disciples see more clearly than masters.
So my father gave over to me. Twenty years later,
as the war spilled out, his death created an avalanche.
First him, then Eva, then Braque and Derain.
Apollinaire, nervous, his head exploding
like a clover leaf, was never the same.
The Tao of history is combat and the urge
to destroy is not a creative urge.

I told Brassai, you're a born draftsman.
You own a gold mine and exploit
only the salt, with this photography
business full of haloes and cosmetic fog.
But he found the world more fraught
with genius than himself and chased
his own tail through Paris for decades.
What bullshit, a peeping Tom blowing

magnesium bombs all through the night,
with Goethe as a guide, posing prostitutes
side by side like potatoes.

Painting is the oldest profession,
best practiced by old men. I remember watching
Goya's fingers in his eighties, trembling as he painted
his last torture scenes, roped to the mountain,
swinging above the ice-fields of his last days,
the chutes, trapdoors, partitions and tunnels,
the hidden places where Death lies waiting.
Painting is praying, and while the street preachers
rub their Bibles and pull their hair
denouncing all sinners, the places we paint
become churches. Why not risk everything?

Dora screamed when I pissed on her bronze head
to improve the patina. She gave it
to a man with a wagon full of pots.
Dora was like that, a beautiful scorpion
that wept as she killed.
I tore her stinger out by the roots.
Women are like cats, their hair
has to be messed up. But these bachelors,
they are wrong. It is good to have a wife.
I suppose it's my mind, so glad to be taken home.

I never married my first model, but Fernande
was the sky to me, an opium dream,
a cloud jumping jagged like a switchblade.
When she appeared I was sitting in my uniform,
decorating the café. I followed her home,
bought a kitten on the way and cradled it,
standing on the doorstep to the Bateau Lavoir
while chestnuts rolled across the porch
and white mice nibbled my canvas.

We have to seize the things we need to create.
When I took Fernande from Sicarde the academic,
he begged for two more weeks. But I wrote a note,
I said I don't give a fuck. When a woman
is yours she is your creation, your equal,
your adversary and will become greater than you
or perish. She and you *are the work*, nothing,
while it lasts, means more. But women
are engines of suffering. Fernande's beauty

held me for a time, but I couldn't stand
any of her little ways. When she sang
it was like a nightingale with a toothache.
Loving someone does not mean we consider them
marvelous, it means we consider them necessary.
When she stormed out, I was already famous.
She took eleven francs and forty bottles of perfume.
She loved and slandered me in equal measure.
Run from a knife, but move in on a gun.

For us Spaniards there's Mass in the morning,
bullfights in the afternoon and brothels
at night, sadness like the Sphinx
where the weathered head becomes an egg,
duende ponderous as a caryatid.
The true confrontation is with the human face,
transparent and flat, like a mask
with eyes of lava, teeth like geraniums
collapsing into frescoes of thistles and cicadas.
For fingers, brilliant yellow and green gladioli
catching softballs of sunlight.

Once in Horta de Ebro, I watched an autopsy
performed with a saw by the night-watchman.

An old woman and her granddaughter
killed by lightning, their sweet faces blackened.
In the elderly gravedigger's shed he sawed
the young girl's head from the top
of the scalp to the nape of her neck,
all the while contentedly chewing on
his unlit blood-soaked cigar.
In the valley, the gypsies with their starved
souls, carved songs from their guitars.

Painting is an instrument of war.
I want to create mountains of paintings,
enough to reach the moon, to express
what no one possesses, to hear the ageless
river throb. My illegitimate battle flag
burns within and without, consumes as it
is consumed. Painting is contagious
and the rosaries of its bones are molded
like the horns of the bull by the matador
peddling backward weightless on the handlebars
of his enemy. Every skeleton, with its wings

stretched out, is a terrific crucifixion
and delicate like forked trees.
God is a very great creator of forms,
but He has no style. The spiders
in my nightmares swarm like skeletons,
shackled like Michelangelo to the ceiling,
like the Viking whom the Christians
threw into a barrel of vipers, shrieking
his war song into the teeth of their Creator.

Nature has to exist so that it may be raped.
I am against everything, everything unknown

is an enemy and if we give spirits a form,
we become free. The mules and cockroaches
do not imitate life, they work as life does,
always on the verge of departure.
Painting makes me do just what it wants me to.
Like Rembrandt who is a tropical forest,
with all the bamboo uprooted and trampled
by elephants. That's how painting erupts,

out of widow's weeds, out of pet shops.
Painting is a very large plow carving its duty
across the terrain of the dispossessed,
a real hodgepodge, like the platypus
or the squirrel that do not know
where they come from or what they are.
I feel and do not decide.
One slaughter follows after another,
processions of totem poles laughing like bear traps.
I do not seek, I find camouflaged

acrobatic flowers bristling with razor blades,
a sunset spreading the confused shadows
of windmills, an owl with the head of a man
cocked beneath a three-cornered hat.
The soul of painting is tension
and perpetual enchantment, to turn
a block of wood into a bird, a toy car
is a baboon's head driving the hunched
shoulders forward. The cat eats the bird.
Picasso eats the cat. Painting eats Picasso.

They just keep coming up, like mismatched cousins,
order and adventure, math and mayhem,
like the scorpion and the owl

hunting among the dusty wild cactus
and rosemary of the Catalan desert,
where all the caves are like doorways
to the interior of the Shadow.
Sometimes when the forms are swarming,
when one form swims over into another form
like sex, the voice of God says do this,
do that, but God is confused and Picasso is not.

II

The Loom at Rest

THE MAYOR OF ANTARCTICA

(for Robert Falcon Scott)

"We shall stick it out to the end and the end cannot be far. It
seems a pity, but I do not think I can write more..."

*last entry of journal found
beside Scott's frozen body, 1911*

The critics believe I am a creature
of commerce, but my diaries are fixed
like an oak in the wind.

When the roof gives way
and the contours quicken,
when the level ice plains stretch far away,

I blunt the horror with the scent
of a woman, chocolate, persimmon,
chamomile are all proven to be

effective against the enemy.
I use the deluge to my advantage
and put out words like a tree springs leaves.

Restlessness is not the culprit,
it is the remedy. The island drifts
and life is that which flows,

but poetry must stand still
for a moment, like a hummingbird,
a circle of pure desire,

an icy breath that rides
on its own melting.
With sulfurous isolation and spine,

I'm building a name. The slow iron
that is my blood is healing into poetry;
but none of this will please my backers.

My investors only pay for the facts.
They say, *I don't know why I'm so lucky.*
The coins just come to my hands.

Like religion, their faith is formless,
it fattens where it stands.
This far South, this base, my flag

frozen in mid-flight like a blue curl;
here I will stake my claim,
shake loose my words, let these long

bloody lines unfurl, the ice
reaching all around me in the dark,
the cracks that break apart this world.

DROUGHT HORSE

(for Degas)

There is no justification for desire,
no trough of logic or swirling word.
The mind goes into the mountain
and out.
>   The hindquarters
>   push the bones ahead,
>   sweeping all taste away,
>   only wind and odor.
Red lizards watching,
>   hook themselves
>   against the rocks.
A woman with a razor
>   in a gray brick building
>   slices her throat
>   from ear to ear.

>   Sand pours down her blouse.

THE DEATH OF THE POET

In a sleepy nation goaded with slogans,
the less ambition you exhibit, the bigger you get.
Ezra Pound was like the Pink Panther at the end,
performing one outrageously stupid act after another.
They gave him *E Pluribus Unum*, right to the sternum,
a door in the face. But up he popped, wise eyes
jutting out of their sockets, unscathed & strutting
in the eleventh hour.

> *You start with a swelled head*
> *and end with swelled feet*, he sd.
> Good Old Ezra, always sd. out loud
> what the others were thinking.

But in the final analysis, the familiar aroma
of the dark forest was no comfort.
Set to frenzy the old panther lost his poise,
betrayed by beauty, bitten to death
in the search for roses,
arriving torn at his destination
only to discover that he'd been there before.
That wonder of wonders, most poetry is formed
from a series of blunders and old Ezra never blinked.
Blackened by the letter bombs, rattled, bedazzled,
he blustered 'til he burst, with an assful of arrows,
wandering more than most.

EXEGESIS

Phil Kaufman
was a yellow dwarf
with a funny walrus mustache
who roomed with Manson
on Terminal Island before Charlie got famous,
who believed that a shared
moment of lightning was a bond,
that a friend will if he can,
that stampeding horses
won't step on a man.
All that mattered to Phil Kaufman,
rummaging through the attics of life,
was a tin star to pin his drunken dreams upon.

Phil made a promise
to burn Gram Parson's body
in the desert,
to cancel the ticket
for his earthly carcass
and create the atmosphere
for a little interstellar travel.
His heart was not corrupted
like the pigs he held suspect
in Clayton County
who were paid to protect
their constituents
and squashed their kosher hearts
by cleaning out the bank,
dropping the empty coffin
in the river's breach,
littering the town's only artery.

Private matters lose their power,
gored happily mad
in the public shortcuts,
forgotten in a dancing spine.
But Gram's last words
were whispered deep in blood,
his sloven majesty threatened.
So Phil did what any true friend would,
upright in the silent hollow,
he took a torch and stood,
a pilgrim in a pilgrim's shadow,
until death, clumsy as a one-armed man,
gripped his coat and pulled.

WASHING LENIN

My father showed me how
to get at the mold
under his arms and behind
his ears. Two or three
times a week we would dip
our sponges in the orange
solution and remove all
the blemishes. Once a year
we carried him in a tank
to the special laboratory
and immersed the great man
in a vat of chemicals.
The body turned blue
then silver then back
to its usual gun-barrel gray
as he lay back on the pillows
so calm, as if he was quietly
meditating. I mean you know
he's dead, but I'm gentle
nonetheless. They knocked over
his giant green statue
and cut it up, but the President
needs me to keep his body clean.
After he died, they removed
his brain and six scientists
scanned it for signs of genius.
They didn't find much.
My father said that Lenin
used to visit him and smoke
a Cuban cigar and laugh
about the snow. I didn't know
how to take this, so I just let

him talk, but last night
the leader of the revolution
walked into my room in his
perfectly pressed suit and stood
at the foot of the bed,
glaring at me, while my wife
jacked him off and quietly sobbed.
After she finished, he unfolded
across the mattress, lay back
between us and fell asleep.
I don't know if this is just
a dream because Olga has been
followed by an emerald sedan
and the driver looks just
like Lenin. I ran to the
mausoleum and there he was
patiently resting while we
age and fret. I don't know,
we're all free now, maybe
it's just my imagination,
but one million peasants
stormed Red Square holding
placards bearing the likeness
of the great leader. Today
I waded through an ocean
of flesh and knelt beside
Lenin's body to begin my chores.
The windows rattled with curses
and denunciations. Burnished
inside this box of chaos, Lenin
was tranquil, his unfurrowed brow
relaxed under my brush and on his
lips, as I dabbed the corner of
his mustache, I swear I detected
the slightest winsome smile.

DEATH IS A FICTION OF STONE

(for Amon Liner)

The driver of jello giraffes
is dead at the wheel,
falling on his horn,
his car like a rocket
covered in maple skin,
symphonies of knives
caressing his neck.
Bumper to bumper,
the gray steel of Justice
has crazed the decaying clocks,
gobbling blue cobwebs
and skull-grains of light.
To mean what you say,
you have to be willing to die,
the smell of your language
smeared on the mirror.
All art aspires to the rhythm
of the day, but there are more gun
dealers in America than gas stations
and we are unhappy in the best
of times. Liberty drifts among
the orange rubber cameras,
segregating the pyramids
of hypodermic skeletons.
The ghoulish adverbs wash their hands
and fall asleep, pelvic-curved
and plastic, syntax spread
across the sunlight.
There is no such thing as Southern poetry.
There is no such thing.

The individual cannot be forced
to flatten the night
with snowflakes of frozen honey.
Flesh and mud meditations
are what I seek, lullabies
of meat and smashed-up stars.
We cannot make time go down
scratching each other's back,
drinking martinis
in the back-lit poverty
of asphalt groves,
spending more money on the prison system
than the school system
while silence grins in the slums,
its eyeholes leaking lime-green dust.
Cathedrals of bees splinter,
a signal that the city has fallen
into flash bulbs of blood.
When the trees begin to speak
and the mind is on fire,
when the snarls of the white hounds
and the white-bearded weeds
swim through the poets
with television fins,
language, like a sonorous animal,
will evolve into its new skin.
Like a dead man walking backward
on glass stilts,
his lizard energy crackling
in the sad air,
a rain of salt statues will wrestle
with death in all its fictions,
in the distance
between necessity and despair.

Exit The Ballets Russes

(for Leger)

Fathered by machines
among mountains of boxes,
the lean ballerinas tip
down the uneven stairs
of the old stage exit
from one century to the next.

Gautier believed the bust
would outlive the State.
Countries come and go, atrocities
attended by gods and monsters.
The tower in Pisa leans
and falls flat.

Our little dance troupe spins
deftly around the rubble.
Ravel squeaks his spoon
across the silver teacup
and fifty slippered feet
hiccup in unison.

Eighteen chimneys honk
in a single city block
like the pipes of a giant organ.
Bassoons squawk, cabs backfire,
the city is an orchestra,
all towers and pistons and smoke.

Behind barred windows,
valets attend to our
ballerinas in repose.
Limbs are oiled, one winces
as she straightens her toes.
The patrons roll like logs

into the street, clog the subway
stations where the trains blink
in greeting one by one and wiggle
off, down into the dark.
In the theater, the last spark

cools behind the stage.
Program pages rustle
with no more tales to tell.
The long sad line of traffic
spans the bridge, postscript
to its own farewell.

THE FATIGUE OF POST-MODERN IRONY

"We believe in ourselves as we do not believe in others. We permit all things to ourselves, and that which we call sin in others is experiment for us...For there is no crime to the intellect..."

—Ralph Waldo Emerson

The Fatigue of Post-Modern Irony

I

The Puritan Dilemma

Once
we built
one hundred
thousand bomb
shelters in
America
trying to
make sense
of the
atom's
terrible
contagions.
We never
used
a one.
Oscar Wilde
said he
knew perfectly
well why
America
was so
violent.
It's because
our wallpaper
was so
ugly.

What is
history
but a
fable
agreed
upon?
The past
is smoke
deep
shadowed
plazas
teeming with
hungry ghosts.
The Puritans
with their
coiled
dilemmas
could not know
that
Father
Incubus
was already
here when
they landed
waiting for
their boats.

II

Forty

Forty
black churches
have burned
in the South
in just
four years.
Thirty years
after
Dr. King
was gunned
down his son
shakes hands
with the
killer
and forgives.
The root
of war
is fear.
Two out
of three
inner-city
black men
in America
are in
prison
or parole.

Forty
percent
of the
water
in North
America
is unfit
for
swimming
fishing
or
drinking.
I saw
a pink
flamingo
plunge
like a
withered
violin
into the
sea.
Olive
trees
quivered
in their
arboretums.

III

Waco Ruby Ridge Oklahoma

What you do
in the karma
kitchen
is your own
business.
This poem
is more
harmless
than
Dioxin
and will spend
less time in
your heart.
In the mission
room twenty
stories above
the high
country
of the swans
my mother
paces clutches
her face
and asks why
I leave out
all the
happy parts.

It is not
enough
to dream
the notes.
You have
to go
inside
your body.
But we are
a bulky
people
hard to move.
It takes
a death
to move
a family
or a
building
in flames
being rammed
by a tank
spooling
on the
lurid
evening
news.

IV

Completely Christian Karate

The local
minister
full of
brimstone
preaches
separation
shaving
the pitch
in the scope
of his
sermon
having caught
a terminal
case of the
millennium
bug using
the tom-tom
time-tested
completely
Christian
tactics
hoping to
karate chop
the teenagers
toward
salvation.

Any man
may call
spirits
from the
dark
but what
will he
say when
they come
and what
will he
do when
they stop?
Tradition
is the
illusion
of
permanence.
It is Xmas
and snowing.
Rudolph
the red-nosed
survivalist
continues to
elude the
FBI.

V

The Black Dahlia

Irony is
the road
to nowhere
but anger
demands
what doesn't
exist
like manifest
destiny
or the
tyranny
of contrition.
Style is
the man
says the rude
psychiatrist
recovering his
repressed
memory
advanced upon
by suicidal
tendencies
a vacant
placability
of black
dahlias.

Falling fast
asleep we
forget that man
is a speck
of evolution
in the
crimson petal
mere by-product
in its
barbed-wire
heart.
The variants
are numberless
melted
into chalk
and ladled
into the yawning
peninsulas.
The bloom
of death
sprouts context
all around
dahlias
run wild
half way
to the sea.

VI

The Hoop Dance

Celebrating
the circle
of life
beneath
a pregnant
golden moon
jumping in
and out of
sacred hoops
the Indians
knew the earth
was round
long before
Columbus
stumbled
into them.
We watch
the cars pass
savage
cabinets
of time
like deer
in the
darkness
blinking our
diamond eyes.

If I
could
speak
to you
as clearly
dear reader
as the
moon speaks
to the hill
I would
lay my
cheek
against
your cheek
and say
this is all
we are
every
blue breath
viewed
from afar
takes
something
from
this
world.

UNDERTOW

Born into darkness, a dog
trained to fight and kill,
tied to the master
and the master's will,
the first quiet vollies droop
across the bowstrings of his eyes.

5,000 people disappear every year,
blotted out by passing strangers
who smiled in greeting
or gently touched their hair.
Lovely meat-filled smiles
see the mad sierras play.

One false move from celebrity,
we get our 15 minutes of fame
by sitting in front of a TV audience
and purging our fathers,
our fucks and our fears,
just as friendly as you and me.

But to murder in volume,
to get your own trading card,
you have to sleep well
at night after having sex
with a corpse.

You have to go into the darkness
and eradicate everything
that is different from you
or loves you
or impedes your movement.

Pushing out, until you
are firmly up above it all
and there is nothing
against your feet,
except the feral testimonies
and pure shadow.

Held aloft by the normalcy
that reflects your speed & precision,
worships the rush of your air,
blown to the aft railing & weightless
in the wake of the great undertow.

Conspiracy Theory

Speck was abducted by a UFO
on the 50TH anniversary of Roswell,
taken from his car while the stereo
blared Wagner's *Ride of the Valkyries*.
Los Vigilantes, the watchers, kept vigil
while Honest John, the pie dog of Mexico,
kept the gophers in their holes.
God said avoid this number
or any combinations thereof,
yet at the end of the Devil's Highway
666, the nation's largest reservation
spills across the desert where Speck
was taken up by heavenly illegal immigrants,
just as he was thinking about Reagan,
the great Satan, crumbling in front of us,
the same cowboy who commanded
Gorbachev to tear down that wall.
Speck felt like he could see it all,
the full fabric of conspiracy,
with his entrails on a cushion
beside him, his life passing before
his eyes on the video screen
clinging to the alien wall.
What kind of culture conducts human
experiments? Speck wondered.
Could they be Nazis or just
federal officials run amok?
Speck was out of the loop when they
tied electrodes to his testicles
to test his spice.
Speck felt himself floating down
a long tunnel of light

and smack into an undiscovered quasar.
Pardon me, ladies, he exclaimed
as he awakened, holding his new
set of teeth in a cup.
Or at least that's what Speck remembered,
before the men in blue showed up.

PRINCIPIA

What if Heidegger met Hawking
and they defeated their singularities?
Uncertainty might bang into the science of risk
and their elementary particles mingle,
giving them pause.

At the temperature
where relativity and gravity intersect,
the universe is a bundle
of noodles unrolling across
an electric field, minute strands
of space-time in high resolution,
many planks vibrating in consummate order,
a symphony immune to any human outcry.

What if Heidegger met Hawking
with a map of the sky,
in some remote outpost
where the warmth of a natural process
was the only brightly-feathered thing?
How many dimensions would be deconstructed,
the patterns on seashells,
the ribbons of arteries, the leopard's spots?

Before two men blink in greeting,
they surmise the other's thoughts.
This is the politics of meaning
when a dying bee sends its signal
to the hive and provokes
the entire colony to attack.

This is the pure system that makes fences,
where the only memory in the mind
of the last man is revenge,
where the moon tangled in the trees
bays like a baby calf for release,
where the odds are fixed,
the stars don't miss a beat,
where Heidegger and Hawking have yet to meet.

The Last Barrier of Sex

In Rio, a mother sits
at her desk and creates
a drama, the country's
most popular soap opera.
Each scene is filled
with the radiance of the
daughter, whose eyes are
her mother's creation.
The daughter, in real life,
is killed by her fictional
lover, stabbed to death
with scissors and dumped
beside the highway. Four
scenes already filmed with
the daughter & her murderer
are given the go-ahead by
the mother, the creator of
the scenes. The country is
hysterical with grief, as is
the mother, who must decide
how her daughter and her
dream-lover-murderer will be
erased from the daily soap
as their characters wheel
back & forth in the media,
leaping tragically in the
unconscious public mind over
the last barrier of sex.

THIRTY YEARS AFTER MY LAI

Thirty years after the bodies
were stacked like cordwood
in the drains, nothing much
has changed. The survivors
cry about the killing that dragged
on for four hours and point
to their grandchildren.

The heirs are grateful
and empty all at once.
Calley and Charlie Company
never asked why, but these hamlets
will always multiply,
mango trees and mosaic pots, huts
that reassemble when the typhoons puff.

Most places are closed, out of season
in the month of blood. We tramped
the bumpy roads between broken ties
and sun-bleached bridges,
rice farmer's hats clumped beside the path
like drowsy white swans.

The snake birds rule the alligator holes,
sucking in the black water, skinny trees
blown like candles to one side.
Dream-building, the villagers
have staked their motor lodge
and crab dock on the marina,
the one part of the island
where the neighbors bite back.

Their beleaguered boats are moored
to the stumps, their vague bows
resisting the flat blue land.
Without a word or worry, the frog chorus
charms the lagoon at twilight,
lobbing the first volley of sound
at the diving birds.

A white shadow passes over
the hissing surf that swallows all.
Underneath the creek of molasses,
where the layers of grief
are inching down, the barons
of the Midway stand and rub their eyes.

STILL LIFE WITH DELIRIUM

"A man must dream a long time to act with grandeur and dreaming is nursed in darkness…"

—Jean Genet

The Paper-Maker's Wave

"Eternity is only the total possession of oneself in a single,
unique moment."

—St. Augustine

In the region of mysterious mosses
and wild genista, among the almond trees,
you are a velvet fish flying.
Your silent impenetrable dignity
is impossible to ridicule,
as invisible as pollen.
Wide eyes in a sudden August rain,
the width of a veil from oblivion.

The stars are swimming in this wind,
an incandescent trellis of flowers
in the quiet avalanche of time.
Like the paper-maker's wave crested
between his hands, the wind flips the sky
and welcomes the lake's serene surface,
unmoved by swallow or salmon strike,
a vast shimmering carpet of silver flies.

There are cliffsides in Montana
where whole dinosaur skeletons lie exposed;
but time is black and this is blue,
this piece of music in you
that I cannot master, a thread of iris
shadow spun and pulled tight between us.
The terrible thing about life
is that we all have our own reasons.

Flickering against the dreaded reversals,
the julep-colored shanties
scroll against the township.
Boat flares set the water on fire and
a pendulum of lava is loosed upon the shore.
My fragments are your reward, and your eyes
are shut tight in the rain,
like dogwood petals folded up in the darkness.

Two Generations of Snow

My friend for all my life,
we flopped and drooled in the crib together,
were weaned bareback on opposite sides
of this filthy creek, where every house
aims their sewage in a straight line.

We waded through the summers
of our youth in Bible School,
so rigid in our native dress,
as we carried the flags
of the Christian and the State,
pledging allegiance to the gray cypress
that hovered crying silver overhead,
clinging to our home runs and our kites.

In high school we flew apart, you,
learning the dark art of narcotics
and moist women, and I, so eager
to please, did not protect you,
never could, not even when we fought
to a draw behind the bus
as everyone cheered and we fell
bloody & exhausted into each other's arms
and knew nothing would ever be
the same as these wild years.

Children of the dirt, we were never given
the aristocratic maxim that a gentleman
may make mistakes but doesn't marry them.
Now you are trapped in your dead
grandmother's house, less than a mile
from where we were born, with a set

of twins and a son of your own,
who begs me, when I visit, for subway tokens
and dreams of riding a bullet train
out of this dead end valley,
straight into the sun.

And even though people keep telling me
how to run my war and that I have forsaken
the South by writing these lines,
I know that Hell is the island where logic
no longer lives and treason is embedded
in the nature of the most beautiful creations,
bubbles on their flowers when they bloom
smiling as I drawl, *thank y'all very much.*

And I cannot explain to my old friend,
as he passes me the joint,
that I am busy giving birth to myself,
that I am enveloped by shame,
spinning a silk which is my pride.
That the elegant strands supporting my betrayal
sink me in a wondrous guilt
and thus I live, poisoned by my own kind,
trapped between two revolutions
in a noble solitude, ingesting the web
of my life a fiber at a time,
the remains of which I spit upon this page.

THE DIASPORA OF STEVEN MANNERS

Everything valuable that I know,
I have learned from women.
They have put me together
with broken buttons and bits of glass,
animal skins and battered hats.

I have lain stoned beneath their blankets,
draped with the madness of celestial telephones.
At times, nourished only on the ether
of my grim formulas, I was told
that nothing would break in here;
that whatever happened, I was ready.

But God's spies know that sex is violent,
that the desert panther, mad to couple,
has the strength of ten tribes,
that sperm rolling inside the rattlesnake
is religious as the daughters of Lot.

That I, with my eyes of mica,
was the lesser twin, stranded at the top
of the canyon, my sins
carefully documented, my body
hissing like a watery balloon.

There will come an evening, I am certain,
while the herds of turtles
row toward their death
with muffled oars, when the last convertible
cruises the beach stuffed with bikinis,

and the last sister is held defenseless
by her wrists on the wrinkled shore.
A fog of men, torn on the strings
of their own instrument,
will make a perfect scream of forgetting,

their progeny glued like smug honey
to the rocks, in the twilight
of dungeons, passing through the slalom
of their automatic doom
on skis of meat.

Emerald sea-flowers will emerge,
their heads ablaze in human forms
and trying to speak.
But then their tortured eyes will meet,
cloaked in feathery remembrance,
of lovers thrown from towers,

of loneliness deep as a needle
in the scattered engines of sleep.
And they will walk slowly together
from the Celtic maze upon a crippled street,
its pathway littered with marble Apollos,
overgrown by the gallows of the beginning.

A Call To Remember

(for Jeff Buckley)

Annoyed, Madam Felicia fanned
the lazy air under one fat fly,
unmoved in the thick Memphis heat.
We listened to the Mississippi hissing
and watched the bloated ropes
jerk tight and roll over
the sandy, potato-colored corpse.
I've spent a decade on the road
shoveling shadows, marooned in a mission
that exchanged one hole for another.

When I was eighteen,
barely a man on a thread,
speech was my father and my great Spain.
In a land beyond the forest,
I muttered my poems alone,
my country grunt breathing
cobwebs on the windowpane.
In the mountain valley
where the Cherokee met the Irish,
my eyes went haywire,
searching for figures in the rain.

A young hawk sits atop the black
walnut tree and listens to my angry wife,
who runs crying across the yard,
holding the naked noise
of her breasts with both hands.
The dogs circle one another in the shade
as I come undone,

peeling my sun-burned face,
fishing the gnats from my lemonade.

Eternally waiting, how can I say what I feel?
How can we know the country
without recovering the lost connections,
the smoky blue silence
beyond the turn in the road?
Let this poem be a call to remember,
the simple repetition of the river,
the song of the stones it turns over,
the bridges that surrender to its load.

AGAMA

All day I pressed the brake
expecting the car to stop
and I lifted a spoon to my mouth
believing no one would waste
the time to poison me.

When I was a child I trusted nothing
and once wrote that I would trade
all the wind for a little rock band
moving the chameleons to sway
under the fat husk of a shivering moon.

And I have, I have paid in blood
for the mute acres of stones,
the theaters of the dunes
that comprise my life:
(Momentary applause like falling water...)

With uncertain little feet
the chameleons creep to the edge
of the road and see what small souls
the people possess to screech away
like colors at the close of light.

Where I live one touch
of a woman's foot passes
unnoticed along my thigh,
but a man's shadow
explodes in the room.

The pedagogue understands,
with his apron of apologies.

The gadfly as well, smeared with deceit.
The snake oil salesman who slips
from city to city in his weird ambulance,
one eye peeled for the police.

A choir of junkies circle
a burning drum, passing a pipe
and offering passersby their bodies,
their flesh transparent as Swiss cheese,
but their harmonies are perfect.

Somehow despair lifts one long string
from the human soul and begs
someone to play it.
Like an empty glove conducting
the orchestra, with the fingers
moving in a silent piaffe;

what is left unsaid matters,
and slices through the parameters of reason.
Like the remaining pieces of the snake
that slide toward one another
even after the rake has rent them apart,

the poet is the priest of the invisible,
roaming inside his hopeless animal,
inviting the carnival, indifferent to protocol.
Like a man probing the covers
for his amputated limb,

I feel the itches and tingles
of the future, the fabric
joined to a soundless form,
phantom limbs where my wings should be,
to master absence is my dream.

LESSONS IN HUNGER

I

Which life is this?
Burned-out in Brooklyn
and my fist is broken again,
the fourth time in a dozen years.
These rituals of the emergency room
are easy to learn, full of spice
or suffering from exhaustion.
But this is new. The doctor speaks no English.
He tells me at 4 a.m., *seet dun heer,*
patting the door with his eager hands.
Beside the boggy red mattress
blood half-fills a beaker.
A silken spray juts across
the ribbed ceiling.
I decide to wait in the hall.
The doctor hands spike at me,
Be still, be still, ah shit.
The bugs busy themselves in the wall.

II

Once before I was born
my mother tried to kill herself,
because my father was going
to leave her.
She rolled out of the moving car
and bounced like a bad apple
on the blacktop.
For two weeks she could not speak,
scorched by rejection,

spitting asphalt into her mint tea
through the cloud of mentholatum.
My father sat in the corner
like an old boot
and croaked for a foot.
My mother's *yes*
was the first word uttered
and made the marrying simple.
In her dimples, my father
turned to wine.
They rubbed the black stone together.

III

In the thirty-six years
that I've known my father,
I've only seen him cry three times.
The first time I was ten
and George Foreman
was pummeling Joe Frazier,
knocked him down six times
in two rounds.
The last was a straight right hand
to the back of Joe's skull,
thrown as he had turned to run,
spasmodically attempting to escape.
He spilled down
like a bowl of jelly,
the fearless eyes frozen
black in the camera.
My father cried, lifted his hand
to hide and I cried too,
because he had,
because in the mad dramatic
clatter of wills I had just

witnessed, something awful
had broken and broken him.
He cradled his beer with both hands
and looked out the window
a long time and there we sat
in that enormous room,
quiet together.

IV

My grandmother died raving mad,
with a tumor the size of a baseball
spreading its fingers in her brain.
My father's voice
had already begun to break
when he summoned me from the road.
My grandmother had fallen
unconscious in the barn,
face down in a swamp of cow shit.

For fifty years she had been
the plow that pulled my grandfather
through his life, birthing three sons
on the kitchen table
and cutting the cord herself.
At 4 a.m. for fifty years
she would rise, pull the eggs
from beneath the chickens
and milk every cow.
My grandfather was up at six,
straight to his plate
of biscuits and bacon strips.
When he ate I never heard him speak.

My grandmother didn't know a soul
when she died, there wasn't
a face she could recognize.
The baby in her womb
was covered in fur, she said.
Moths were flying in her chest,
spreading their wings in her head.
She crawled on all fours
and hid in the closet,
ate the lint from beneath her bed.

When she died, my father and I
were on opposite sides,
each of us held a hand.
The room was filled
with her last sigh,
like a lily that breaks on the water
in a sudden bubble
and then the long horrid whine
of hospital machinery
with nothing left to do.
No, my father said, and fell
to his knees trembling and crying
in a lost sea, washed like a crab
from a rock, swimming in mid-air
through white static.
Boys help, he said,
as the doctors and the family
crashed into the room,
each more frantic than the other.

My father and I handle crisis
the same, we have to be alone.
I watched him the rest of the night,
huddled in the darkness
with the eyes of a mountain,

as the small humiliations piled up,
the taboos of the bathroom,
the silence of the kitchen table,
the endless aphasia
like a cage against love.
I don't know who you are,
he said to me.
I don't know what happened to the time.
My father slept through my childhood
in a trance on the couch,
an exile in his own house.

I drifted upon the rickety fire escape
and traced with my fingertip
the imagined outline
of my grandmother's spirit,
like a dusty bee bumping across
the alley, creeping to the outskirts
of the hospital, her golden figure
reflected in seven empty windows,
in a building set next to nothing.
A mall once, a tackle shop
behind bars, a haberdashery
with a giant velvet glove
painted on the door, waving
as my grandmother passed over,
like a wind trail on the water,
and then the wrinkles are gone.

V

I'm home now, like Frost,
the place where,
when you have to go there,
they have to take you in.

My father has stopped drinking.
His second attempt in thirty-five years.
He descends the stairs, shaking so bad
that he begs me for a joint.
But I'm penniless, with a broken fist,
so I have to stay sober.
And I realize that my father
has been drunk his whole life
for the same reason.

I light his cigarette instead.

CRITICAL MASS

(for Aimee)

One minute past noon
and all is darkness,
except for you.
The cats prowl electric in the field.
The hammock ropes dangle,
free from burden.
And what a strange smell,
two lives burning together.

What animal is this
we are making that
steals our breath?
That rushes to rescue
our fragments?
We were not sent here
to save each other.
We were meant to comfort.

But what parts of my skin
can I give to you?
On what plot will you
build your dreams?
In the arms of the light
a solitary spirit
begs and growls
for us to hold our own.

In all crisis, opportunity.
In all bedlam, beauty.
Our hands are older

than our bodies,
creased with maps
of secret history,
of every hushed liaison,
every tearful turning away.

Just as the land is revealed
to be older than its people
when the mosaics speak,
my voice is only one
of the forces of the world.
But make no mistake,
as I am all men in you,
my words are a storm.

The wind that I blow
into you will seek
the water in your leaves.
The anger that I push
like a raisin
into the cake of your body
will spread and thicken.
All past and present

will stick to us,
be swallowed into us
as we float like black holes,
forgetting into the future,
until all time is us and now,
the way the novas dance
in their final seconds, all planets
revolving together into night.

The Acquired Inability To Escape, Inverted

I have decided to learn and let live.
Everybody thinks I am a fool anyway.
My leaving has been inverted;
it's always right now until it's later
in the jagged residence of horseshit and hysteria.
I have failed. I am slowly destroying myself
with friendly fire, with ill-timed remedies
and mission creep. But it's quiet here.

It seems to me, cultural particulars aside,
when I have been *all that,* during spells
of arrested development, nothing started.
Page by page, I have reduced my biography
to a single instruction while the halogen
lamp is slowly cooking ladybugs
as physics fails them. *Breathe,* I say.

All my friends are hermits, pigeon-toed
and sprawling, with salmon-colored eyes.
The thought that we might cease to exist
is not hell enough with our bellies full.
In this age of perceived faith,
any island will do, traipsing
where famous men have fasted.

We are all black now or to come
and it doesn't matter if the enemy is within,
dripping with frantic libido.
We are either born black
(curiously contagiously neglected)
or turn black when we die.
Now I am white, with cooked women in orbit.

The sky is raining orange peels,
steaming, with its wheels collapsed.
I'm ragged and go off today,
blown to pins and limping,
pausing to hug my iron-gray brother
as we pass along the road.

DREAMING OF SEGOVIA

I got a girl who dreams of Segovia,
who takes the long view
from the Henry River,
who sees in her ascension of bliss,
four shades of blue mountain mist

hanging in a vacuum like the sun,
framing the faces of the sky,
like Spanish shrouds in Barcelona
surrounding the poor mothers,
cluttered in the groin of Gaudi's cathedral.

She coddles the cougars
and breaks the rabbit's neck,
pooh-poohs the vulgar ape
and floats upon his smoke,
sniffing out the diptherias of ignorance.

A hunter of the morning star,
it is for nothing that she grazes
the cricket's horn and shovels
shit calmly, to say *hello* to the wren;
she suffers merely to say *hello*.

Medicinal blossoms of bloodroot
bloom nearby and what do our enemies
see when she is leveled by this rare find,
transfixed in the trees,
her fierce blue eyes ablaze with sky?

The day after Thanksgiving
we witnessed a lunar eclipse.
We saw three owls hunting
mice in the moonlight;
their wings were blades.

All the people, like driftwood,
were called from the mall
to gather on the ridge,
their cars abandoned,
shoved to the side of the road.

The trees were bursting with little v's,
pointing in unison toward the summit
of Mt. Mitchell, its peak an edge,
a diamond routinely wasted
in gardens of light.

A giant black panther,
floating upside down,
was hiding its two faces
from the moon, now silver
and flush before the fade.

Flying past Glass Mine Falls,
its claws frozen in a perfect reach,
the great cat leaped into the watery window
in the middle of the shadows,
five thousand feet above the sea.

At this altitude
two hundred years ago,
the last buffalo was killed
in the Blue Ridge mountains
by a bored settler named Joseph Rice.

At this altitude, on the other side
of the world, a thousand men
in a ship shaped like a wedge,
were chasing a glacier, with shooting stars
blown round in their hair.

Their fingers knotted
beneath the changing moon,
listening intently
as an elephant choir
rose from the mist,

raising their horns aloft
and dreaming of Segovia,
just like me and my girl
on a mountainside drenched with dew,
guitar safaris unfurling in our heads.

A Psalm for Camille

(born July 14, 1998)

First of all, little one,
let me tell you about life.
Everything I have said
that I would never do
I have done.

I decided early on
that no one was happy all the time.
There are slivers of happiness,
needles of momentary joy
that enter your life
with a flush poke-through.

And everyone knows
that to find a needle
in a haystack,
you have to burn
the whole damn thing.

The dogs of war, Camille,
are just deaf old men
with accordions, puffing and squawking
for a patch of street corner
to call their own.

In every mirror
there is a dove waiting
to swim into your heart.
That is your mother singing.
Your father is the echo of his father,

a cliff along the coast
covered in birds.

Drawn by the knot-holes in the beach,
giant crabs and blind crustaceans
are wading from the surf
into the sun-split salt deposits
and the fierce mineral silence.

This is the place of angels, little Camille,
everywhere the invisible mouth
may suck, deep and slow.
In these caverns, your grandmother
and aunt point delightedly
and they know.

They smell the spray that paints
their faces with pearls.
The same salt pearls
poured out of the deepest well
when you were born,
gushing like a new river.

The tiny cherry that was your life
bobbed like a red cork in the storm.
Counting your fingers and toes,
we vowed to love you forever
and your little wax lips kissed
us every one, like a tiny candle
passing its flame from mouth to mouth.

In a sea of blood, Camille,
you are the wild plum
that will find root in the rock.
You are our northernmost star,

covered in golden leaves
and shining like a new mandolin.

Always speak the secret language
of the worms and the squid.
Put your soul where you want
and never doubt these lines.
In circles we will sing your story
and be restored, a family at last,
finding its orbit in your eyes.

NOTES

THE PINK RIVER DOLPHINS OF PERU

Pythia—the priestess of Apollo who delivered the oracles

THE POWER OF MOVEMENT IN PLANTS

Title taken from an essay by Charles Darwin

BRACE'S ROCK

Fitz Hugh Lane—(1804-1865) American painter and father of
the art movement known as luminism

RUDY

Rudolf Nureyev—(1938-1993) Russian defector and ballet
master who died of AIDS complications.
"bowed eighty-nine times in Vienna" (Guinness Book of
World Records) record for curtain calls after a performance.
"The sea howl and the sea yelp,
are different voices often
together heard."
The Dry Salvages—T.S. Eliot, 1941

NARCISSISYPHUS

"For the listener, who listens in the snow,
And, nothing himself, beholds
Nothing that is not there and the nothing that is."
The Snow Man—Wallace Stevens, 1923

The Painter as Mantis Sings the Blues

Many quotes herein attributed to Picasso by Andre Malraux (*Picasso's Mask*, 1974)
"Run from a knife, but move in on a gun."
—Jimmy Hoffa

The Mayor of Antarctica

Robert Falcon Scott—(1868-1912) A British explorer of the South Pole whose entire company was lost on the return trip. "Poetry should ride like an ice cube on its own melting."
—Robert Frost

Exegesis

Gram Parsons—(1946-1973) American country-rock singer whose music was highly influential and merged several genres. During the funeral ceremony for Gram's close friend Clarence White, Gram was overheard stating that when he died, rather than being buried in the ground, he would like to be taken out to The Joshua Tree desert of southern California and burned. After Gram died in The Joshua Tree Inn, his body was taken to the Los Angeles International Airport in preparation for being flown to Louisiana for burial. Gram's road manager Phil Kaufman and a friend, Michael Martin, got very intoxicated, borrowed a broken down hearse and drove to LAX to retrieve the body. After crashing into a wall and almost being arrested, Phil took Gram's remains into the desert, poured gasoline inside the coffin and set him ablaze. The two were arrested several days later and fined $700.00 for stealing and burning the *coffin* (it was/is not against the law to steal a dead body). Gram's partially burned remains were finally laid to rest in a modest cemetery near New Orleans, Louisiana.

Washing Lenin

Vladimir Ilyich Lenin—(1870-1924) Russian revolutionary and premier whose body was mummified upon his death and is still displayed in Moscow.

Death Is a Fiction of Stone

Amon Liner—(1940-1976) American poet who died prematurely from a congenital heart defect.
"to mean what you say, you have to die" —Virgil

Exit the Ballets Russes

Fernand Leger—(1881-1955) French modernist painter
Maurice Ravel—(1875-1937) French composer

The Puritan Dilemma

Title taken from a biography by the same name of John Winthrop, written by Edmund S. Morgan, 1958

Waco Ruby Ridge Oklahoma

"Rudolph the red-nosed survivalist" is Eric Rudolph, accused of bombings at the Olympics in Atlanta, GA and listed among the FBI's Ten Most Wanted. He remains at large.

The Black Dahlia

"Now sleeps the crimson petal, now the white;
now droops the milk white peacock like a ghost."
—Alfred, Lord Tennyson

Principia

Martin Heidegger—(1889-1976) German philosopher and leading proponent of existentialism
Stephen Hawking—(1942-) British physicist whose work is an attempt to unify General Relativity with Quantum Theory.

Thirty Years After My Lai

On March 16, 1968, a company of American soldiers led by Lt. William Calley, killed 504 of the 700 villagers in the hamlet of My Lai, located near Vietnam's central coast. Calley was court-martialed and sentenced to life in prison in 1971. He was paroled three years later and now runs a jewelry store in Columbus, GA. His murder conviction was overturned in 1999.

The Diaspora of Steven Manners

"religious as the daughters of Lot"
Lot was the nephew of Abraham. His wife was changed into a pillar of salt for looking back during their flight from Sodom. Later he was seduced by his daughters while drunk and impregnated them. Their offspring became the leaders of two different tribes in Canaan, the Moabites and the Ammonites. (Genesis 19:30-38)

A Call To Remember

Jeff Buckley—(1966-1997) American singer and songwriter who killed himself in Memphis by leaping into the Mississippi River at night.

AGAMA

a genus of lizards that can change the color of their skin.
Also, from Sanskrit, the Tantric writings which announce the
arrival of knowledge.
"The poet is the priest of the invisible."
—Wallace Stevens

DREAMING OF SEGOVIA

Andres Segovia—(1893-1987) Spanish classical guitarist and
composer.
"poor cluttered in the groin of Gaudi's cathedral"
—Antoni Gaudi i Cornet—(1852-1926) Spanish architect
whose masterwork, La Sagrada Familia, remains unfinished in
Barcelona.

Keith Flynn is the founder and managing editor of *The Asheville Poetry Review*, which was established in 1994. He studied at Mars Hill College and the University of North Carolina—Asheville, winning the Sandburg Prize for Poetry in 1985. He moved to Nashville, TN in 1987 and formed the nationally acclaimed rock band, *Crystal Zoo*, which has produced three albums: *Swimming Through Lake Eerie* (1992), *Pouch* (1995), and the forthcoming *Nervous Splendor* (2001). Serving as lyricist and lead singer, Flynn was twice awarded the Emerging Songwriter Prize from the American Society of Composers, Authors and Publishers (ASCAP) in 1991 and 1992. His poems have appeared in scores of journals and anthologies around the world including *The Carolina Quarterly, The Colorado Review, The Cuirt Journal (Ireland), Defined Providence, New Millennium Writing, Word and Witness: 100 years of North Carolina Poetry, Poetry Wales, Earth and Soul: The Kostroma Anthology* (Russia), *Rattle*, and *The Southern Poetry Review*. He is author of two previous collections of poetry: *The Talking Drum* (Metropolis Communications, 1991) and *The Book of Monsters* (Urthona Press, 1994). In 1996, second editions of his first two books were published and Flynn was awarded the Paumanok Poetry Prize. He lives with his wife, Aimee, in Marshall, North Carolina.

About this Book

This book was set in Monotype Bembo which was based on typefaces cut by Francesco Griffo for the printing of *De Aetna* by Aldus Manutius in Venice in 1495. *De Aetna* was written by Pietro Bembo about his trip to Mount Etna. Griffo's design is considered one of the earliest of the Garalde Oldstyle typefaces which were the predominant text types in Europe for 200 years from the early sixteenth through the seventeenth centuries. The Oldstyle Roman typefaces are still widely used in contemporary texts because of their classic beauty and high readability. Stanley Morison supervised the design of Bembo for the Monotype Corporation in 1929. The italic of this typeface is modeled on the handwriting of the Renaissance scribe Giovanni Tagliente.

♾ The paper in this book is recycled and meets the guidelines for permanence and durability of the Committee on Production Guidelines for Book Longevity of the Council on Library Resources.

Special thanks to
Lowell Allen and M. Gunner Quist
for help designing the cover.

*This book was printed
in the United States of America
by Thomson-Shore, Inc.*

www.irisbooks.com